Carry On, My Friend...

Life Is Waiting

Linda J. Paige

Carry On, My Friend... Life Is Waiting

Copyright © 2020 Linda J. Paige.

Produced and printed by Stillwater River Publications.

All rights reserved.

Written and produced in the United States of America.

This book may not be reproduced or sold in any form without the expressed, written permission of the author and publisher.

Visit our website at **www.StillwaterPress.com** for more information.

First Stillwater River Publications Edition

Library of Congress Control Number: 2020908691

ISBN: 978-1-952521-16-4

1 2 3 4 5 6 7 8 9 10
Written by Linda J. Paige
Book design by Emma St. Jean
Published by Stillwater River Publications
Pawtucket, RI, USA.

Publisher's Cataloging-In-Publication Data
(Prepared by The Donohue Group, Inc.)

Names: Paige, Linda J., author.
Title: Carry on, my friend ... : life is waiting / Linda J. Paige.
Description: First Stillwater River Publications edition. | Pawtucket, RI, USA : Stillwater River Publications, [2020]
Identifiers: ISBN 9781952521164
Subjects: LCSH: Hope--Quotations, maxims, etc. | Perseverance (Ethics)--Quotations, maxims, etc. | Gratitude--Quotations, maxims, etc.
Classification: LCC PN6308.H66 P35 2020 | DDC 808.882--dc23

*The views and opinions
expressed in this book are solely
those of the author and do not necessarily
reflect the views and opinions
of the publisher.*

Dedication

To my loving grandmother,
Mary Barros, who raised me.
Her love and perseverance were never ending.
She gave me the love of reading and music.
I will always miss her.

To my dad, Gregory A. Andrade,
who taught me discipline and perseverance.
I've seen you go through a lot in your lifetime
and you have persevered through it all.
Thank you for your love and patience.
May God bless you today and always.

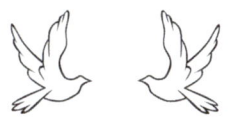

Table of Contents

1. Perseverance 3
2. 'Attitude' of 'Gratitude' 7
3. Smile 15
4. Retreat 19
5. Lily 'Ma' Carter 22
6. The Love of Reading... The Love of Music 26
7. This Too Shall Pass (Part One) 30
8. This Too Shall Pass (Part Two) 34
9. Procrastination 38
10. Don't Give Up 43

Acknowledgments 47
About the Author 53

Lord,
make me an instrument
of Your peace.
Where there is hatred,
let me sow love;
where there is injury, pardon; where
there is doubt, faith;
where there is despair, hope;
where there is darkness, light; where
there is sadness, joy.
O, Divine Master,
grant that I may not so much seek
to be consoled as to console;
to be understood as to understand;
to be loved as to love;
for it is in giving that we receive;
it is in pardoning that we are
pardoned; it is in dying that we are
born again to eternal life.

PRAYER OF ST. FRANCIS

Do all the good you can,
By all the means you can,
In all the ways you can,
In all the places you can,
At all the times you can,
To all the people you can,
As long as you ever can.

JOHN WESLEY

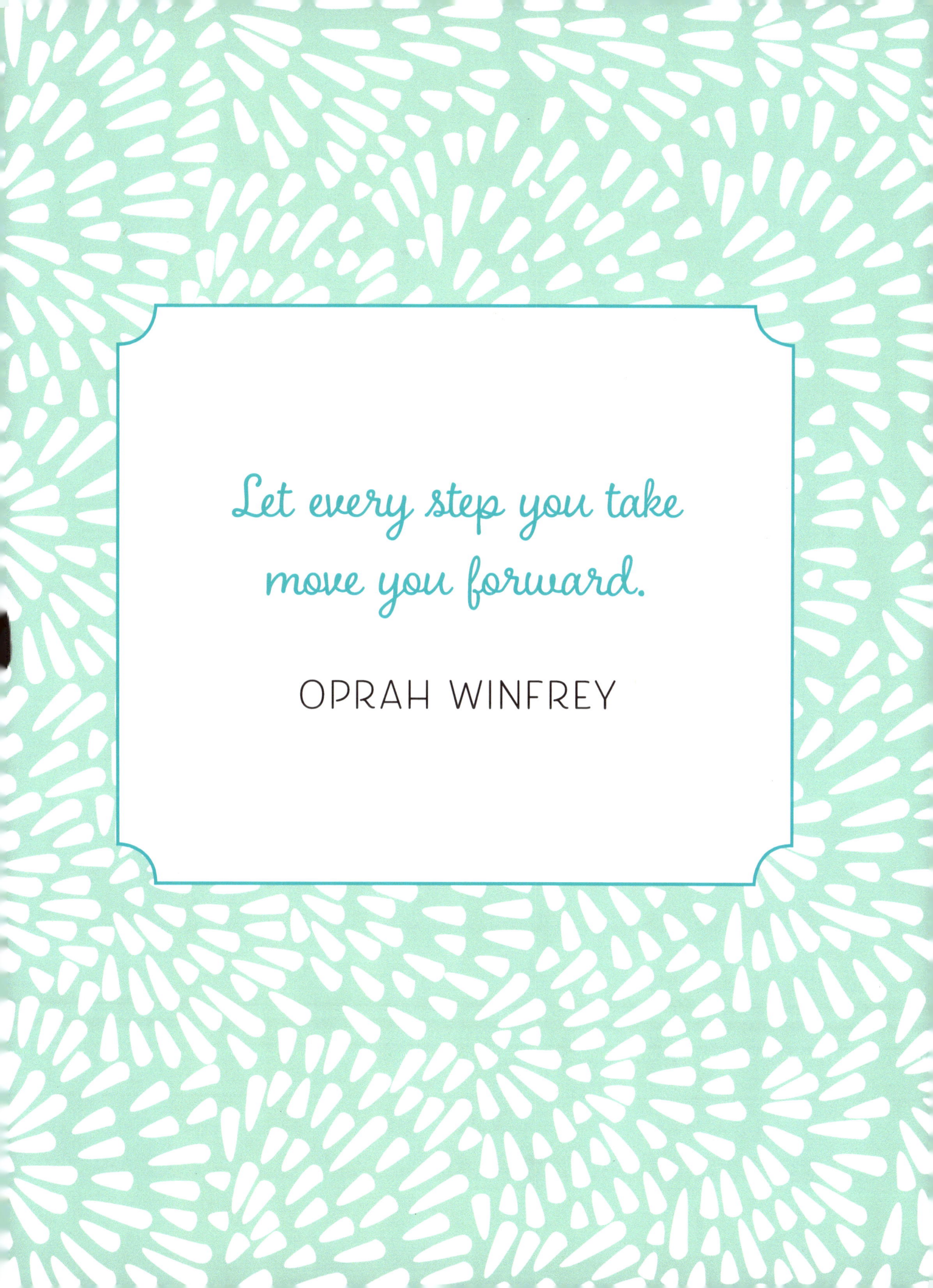

CHAPTER 1
Perseverance

This is my favorite word in the English language. Every so often I review my journals and see 'perseverance' in many forms. Especially on days that are not so good. Yes, I have my days too when I can't seem to put one foot in front of the other... but I do.

I also know in my heart of hearts that this 'putting one foot in front of the other' is not of my own doing. It is of God. Left to my own devices... I would not start my day. I would be 'stuck' in bed or la-la land wherein nothing gets done.

Perseverance is important to me, and means that yes, I am making progress. I am moving about and have my being. Yes!

For the most part, I feel that society perseveres because I like to people-watch and they are on the move. I have spoken to people who felt ill a certain day and yet... they're moving. They're persevering. It's amazing how we as a people can keep moving 'no matter what' sometimes with pain... sometimes with burdens that we carry but the important fact is... we're persevering.

So I encourage you, my reader to 'persevere'... move ahead and see what the day brings about for you.

CHAPTER TWO
'Attitude' of 'Gratitude'

Hello? Oh, there you are! Now that I have your attention, how are 'you' doing today? Hopefully, all is well. If not, don't despair. There is still 'hope' for all of us. Persevere and don't give up... most things in life 'do' pass and a better day returns. Yes! The sun 'will' shine again, birds 'will' sing, friendships and healing 'will' return.

How do I know these things? From my own personal experience. And so now you may be thinking to yourself: 'where am I going with all this thinking? What is this about birds singing again, the sun shining, friendships, healing and better days? Maybe, just maybe in this day and age, all of the above-mentioned 'positive' situations cannot be. But, again from my own life experiences, I say 'yes!' it can be.

Hello, are you still there? Good. Stay with me just a bit while I elaborate. My thinking in the aforementioned is about my 'attitude of gratitude' to life and all it has to offer me. For example, yesterday I was calmly sitting waiting patiently for the RIPTA bus when I looked up to the heavens and just felt such a sense of serenity. I felt so alive and I really wanted to shout to the heavens (luckily, I was able to keep myself under control, lest I frighten other passengers waiting) and just bubble over with joy from within my soul.

You see, I really enjoy days like this when I'm actually 'grateful' to be alive. I remember a time in my life when I was 'not' so 'grateful.' Everything and everybody was getting on my last nerve. I mean, really, I only had one nerve left as it was! It seemed to me that everyone was stepping on that one nerve (ouch!). But then wouldn't you know it, a better day 'did' come along! The next day, to be exact.

There I was just sleeping and getting the rest I so needed to start my day and guess what? Birds came along and started singing (at 6 am!) Now, mind you, at first I felt aggravated because this one particular bird was singing the same chorus over and over. I'm thinking to myself: "doesn't this bird know any other song or at least a different verse?" Yes...for a minute I had an 'attitude.' I don't like waking up with an 'attitude' if I can help it. So you know what I did? I changed my 'attitude' to 'gratitude.' Yes, that little bird was 'getting on my last nerve' but hey, at least I could hear him! I felt 'grateful' for hearing because some people in this world cannot hear and miss the finer things of life such as birds, music, conversation, children's laughter, etc.

Another reason for my 'attitude of gratitude' is for the friends I have in my life that understand me and really accept me for who I am. Especially on those days when I don't feel quite like myself. Truly I've been blessed to have many people cross my life who really helped me get through the day. For example, a laugh here and there, words of encouragement, etc. God bless them one and all.

In closing, let me recap. An 'attitude' of 'gratitude' can really help one get through the day. At least it has for me. It changes my whole outlook on life, people, situations, etc. Just the little things in life can uplift my spirits and allow me to feel appreciation.

So my friend, look to the heavens, birds, trees, waters or whatever helps you unwind and feel the 'ripple of gratitude.' It's a great feeling!

All it takes is one kind word to nourish another person.

FRED ROGERS

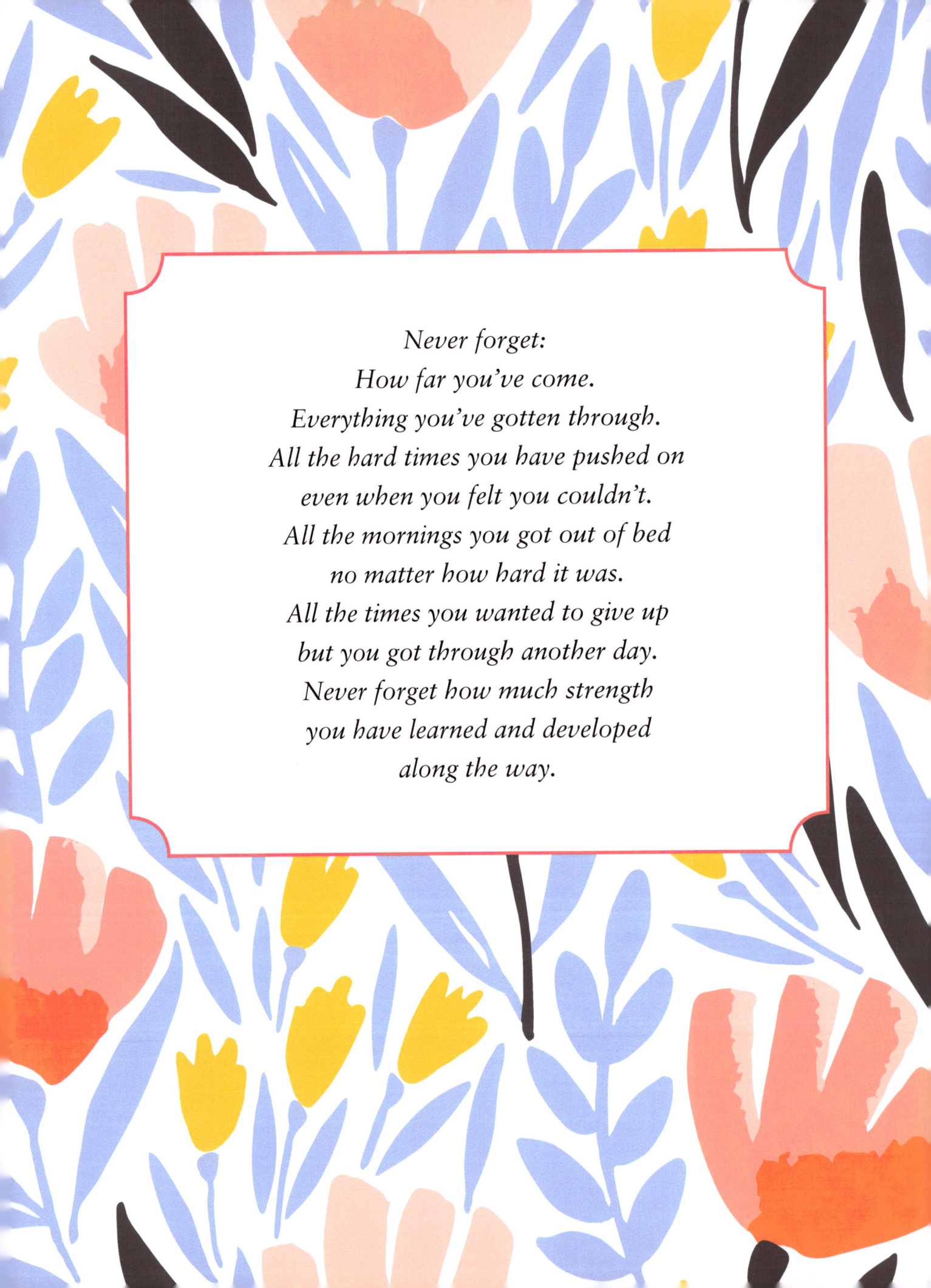

Never forget:
How far you've come.
Everything you've gotten through.
All the hard times you have pushed on
even when you felt you couldn't.
All the mornings you got out of bed
no matter how hard it was.
All the times you wanted to give up
but you got through another day.
Never forget how much strength
you have learned and developed
along the way.

CHAPTER THREE
Smile

I would like to share about a 'smile' and what it can do for the soul and spirit. For example... I was going to catch the bus to my next destination when this person smiled at me and I smiled back. I see this gentleman just about every day during my travels. And he always has a smile for me and I, likewise, smile back. This makes my day brighter as I hope my smile too has brightened his day.

In observations of my daily routine I run into many people and some of these people are hurting in one way or another. Physical, emotional, financial, spiritual. I, of course, want to 'reach out and help' in any way I can but most of what I can do is just... pray. God, please comfort them as you see fit. Believe it or not, often times the next time I see them, they look brighter and walk taller. Yes, even a smile breaks through.

It's like on a cloudy day... and... then... the sun shines through the clouds! Yes! For me it does wonders. I hope it helps to lift the spirits of others too!

So, my friend, if and when you can...smile...see and feel the difference in your day. Trust me, it works!

A goal is not always meant to be reached; it often serves simply as something to aim at.

BRUCE LEE

CHAPTER FOUR
Retreat

I had the privilege of attending a women's spiritual retreat earlier this year, and I must say, it was great!

From the time I walked in the doors until I left the premises, I felt such a sense of peace and tranquility. Even nature was at peace.

This was my fourth time attending this particular retreat, and I would love to go again in the near future. It was a great getaway from the stresses of life.

The other facet of the retreat was... organization. Everything was timed to a 't' with plenty of breaks included for quiet time, reflection and rest time. Food was also served and tables were set in a very professional manner with everything a person needed right there within reach.

I encourage all who can to 'take a retreat' away from the 'hustle and bustle' of life. It is so refreshing!

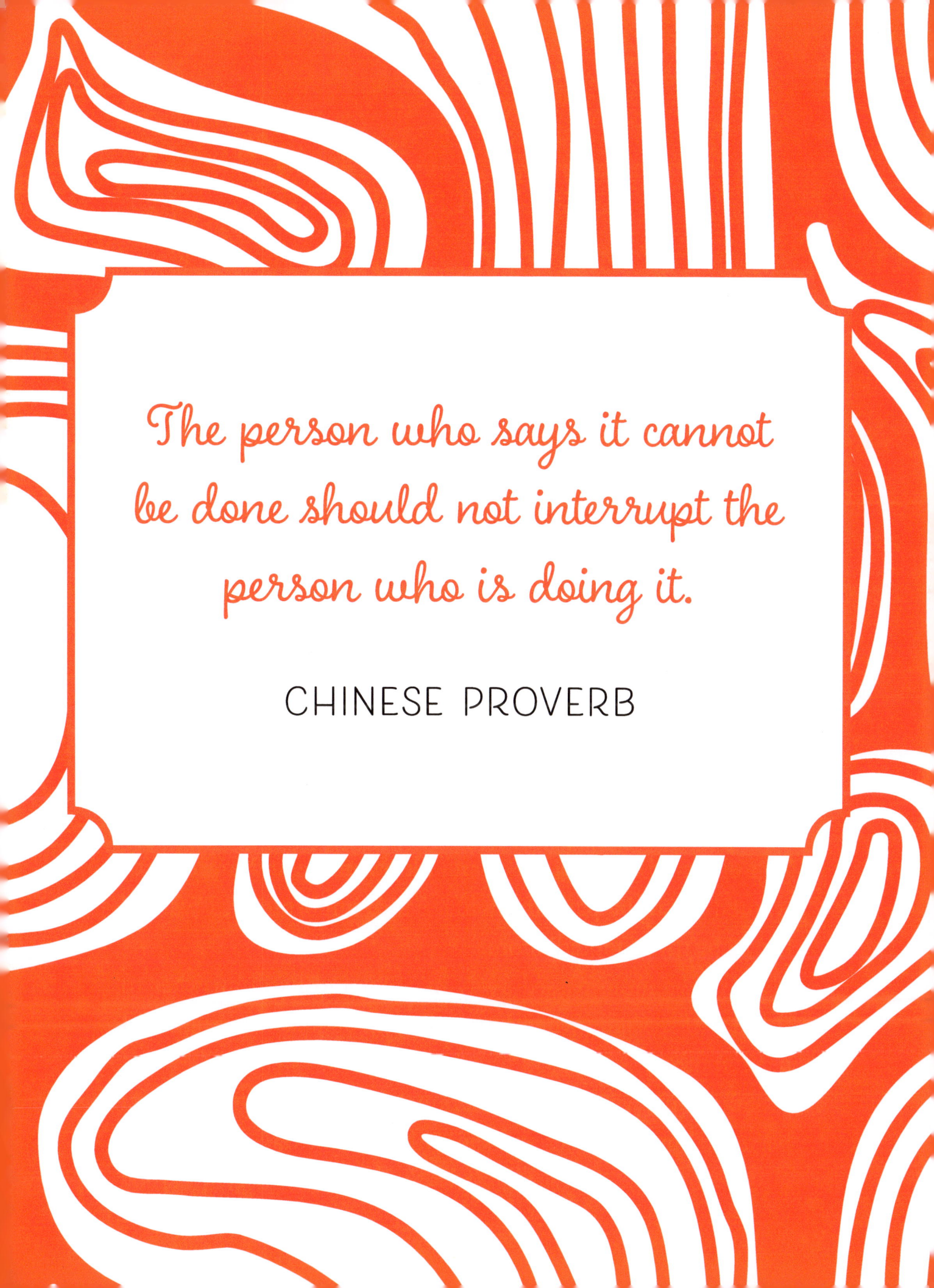

The person who says it cannot be done should not interrupt the person who is doing it.

CHINESE PROVERB

CHAPTER FIVE
Lily 'Ma' Carter

I met Lily Carter back in 1989 when I moved here to Providence. At the time she was 'first lady' of a church on the east side of Providence. Also, we were members of the same church. I knew from the start that I would want her to be a friend of mine. You see, reader, I admire any person who can carry themselves in a calm fashion and so this is how it was with Lily.

She is a very calm person and carries herself in that way. She also has a very professional, neat appearance at all times. I admired her from day one.

This is another blessing in my life that I am grateful for. As I observed her over the years, I knew more and more that I wanted her to be part of my life. More importantly, I wanted her to be my 'adopted' mom.

My own mom passed away in 1986 and I still miss her to this day. Especially when I am going through something and I need 'motherly advice.'

So as time went on and I became closer and closer to Lily, I began to bond with her and she with me. One day on a Sunday morning after church I took her aside and told her how much I admired her. I then asked if she would become my 'adopted' mom... and... she said 'yes!' I was so happy! I almost did cartwheels around the neighborhood! But I didn't.

So I have known Lily for thirty years now and I couldn't ask for a better 'adopted' mom... ever! She is still calm after all these years and extremely patient with me. Another blessed quality that she has is listening skills. Like my own mom, she gives me her undivided attention and listens to every word I say. Her understanding of my moods is truly phenomenal. Lily has been with me through my ups and downs. She is a true friend!

May she forever be blessed today and always.

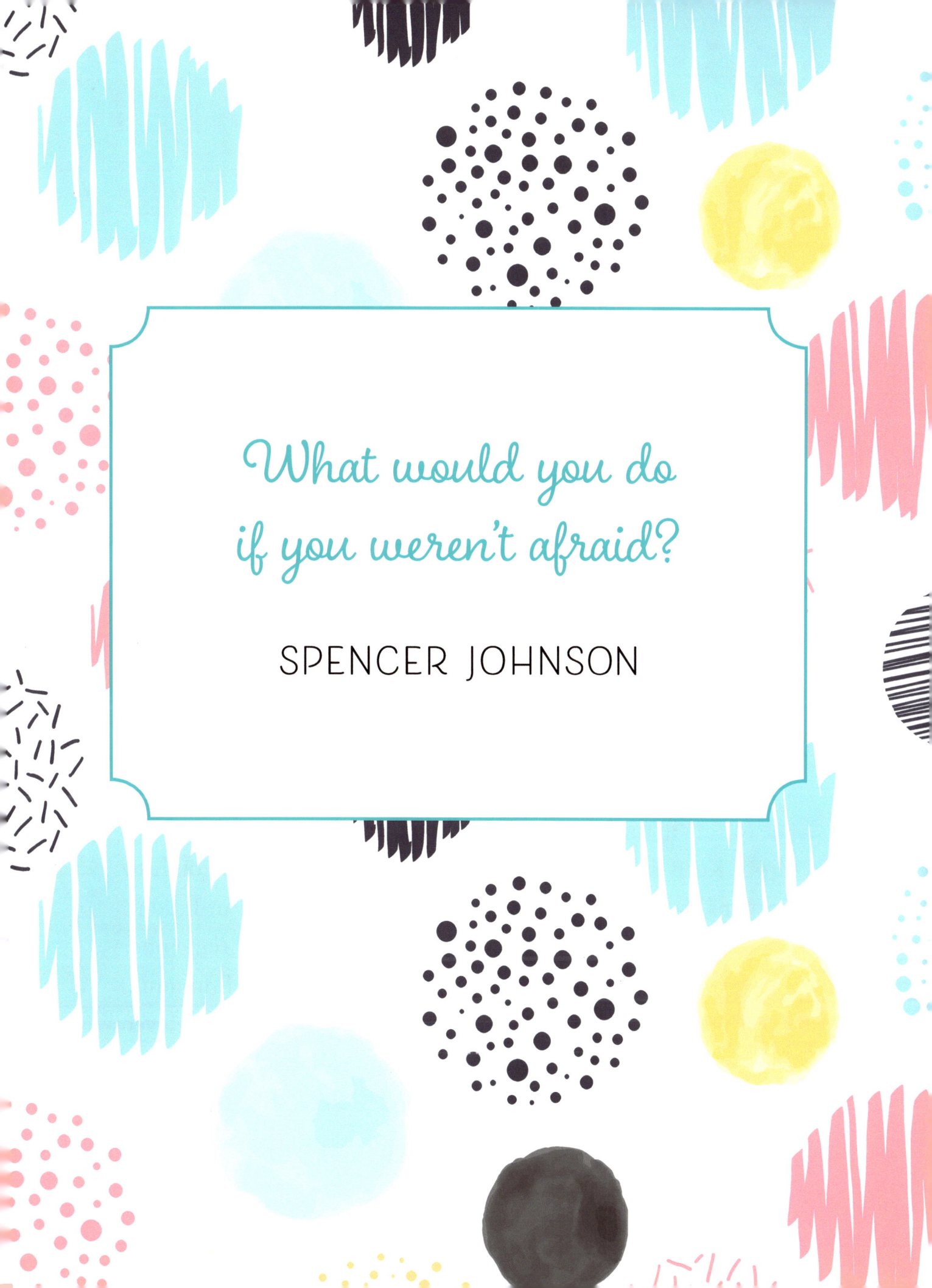

CHAPTER SIX
The Love of Reading... The Love of Music...

I can't say which one I love more. Reading or music because I seem to love them both. As stated in a previous chapter, my grandmother gave me the love of reading as a teenager and well into my adulthood, I am still reading!

Not only did she teach reading to me, but then there was music to enjoy. Today, I enjoy different genres of music. The one I am most familiar with would be... gospel. My grandmother had me singing in the 'little people's' chorus at the tender age of five. I still enjoy singing 'til this day. She then encouraged me to sing in the 'glee club' at school. My first solo was: "Raindrops Keep Falling on My Head." I can't begin to tell you how nervous I was to sing in front of the whole school! But I did it!

It seems strange that as a five-year-old I don't remember being so nervous. But as a teen it's a different story. Hmmmm...

Anyway, my grandmother continued to encourage me even though my nerves were 'on edge' each time I had to sing a solo. I actually had a panic attack! Back then I didn't know it was that. All I know was my stomach hurt along with other discomfort.

Also, in my teen years I joined a church and I sang in the 'gospel choir.' We went on to make a recording of which I was very proud. My grandmother was also in this choir. This was back in 1976.

As time went on, I sang in different church choirs as well as doing solos. I would also sing for different occasions such as weddings, funerals, celebrations, family birthday parties, etc. I still would become nervous but have used coping skills to help 'calm my nerves.'

Thank God for my grandmother who didn't give up on me. No matter how nervous I was, she would pray with me and encourage me to 'use my God-given talent.'

Music is one of the blessings in my life that I could never forget because God has given me the gift to sing, and I want to sing 'songs of praise and encouragement' to help somebody along the way. In the same way that I have been 'blessed' when someone else sang... whether solo or in a choir.

So, my reader, if you have any kind of musical talent to share with the world... Do it! Yes... you may feel nervous at first but try singing to family members first, then maybe your friends, then branch out from there as you feel more courage to do so. You will be just fine! Try it!

Be not afraid of growing slowly; be afraid of only standing still.

CHINESE PROVERB

CHAPTER SEVEN
This Too Shall Pass (Part One)

Thank you, lord, for another day and bringing me thus far in this day...

According to my previous journal entries, many things in my life have passed and so will the loss of this job.

I can't say that I don't have feelings about this turn of events because I do but I also know in time... this too shall pass.

Sitting here thinking about Yolanda Adams' song... "This Too Shall Pass"... and it is so true because as written earlier many, many things in my life have passed and I'm still here by the grace of God.

I'm going through many different feelings but I know in my heart of hearts that... **This too shall pass.**

I can even use different examples in my life to help encourage people to 'press on' because **this too shall pass.**

No, I have never been homeless or out on the streets, but I still believe that in time... housing will come forth... and... **This too shall pass.**

Life throws all kinds of things our way, and when we can't stand the pain no longer... there is hope... this too shall pass.

Be strong my sister... be strong my brother... for **this too shall pass.**

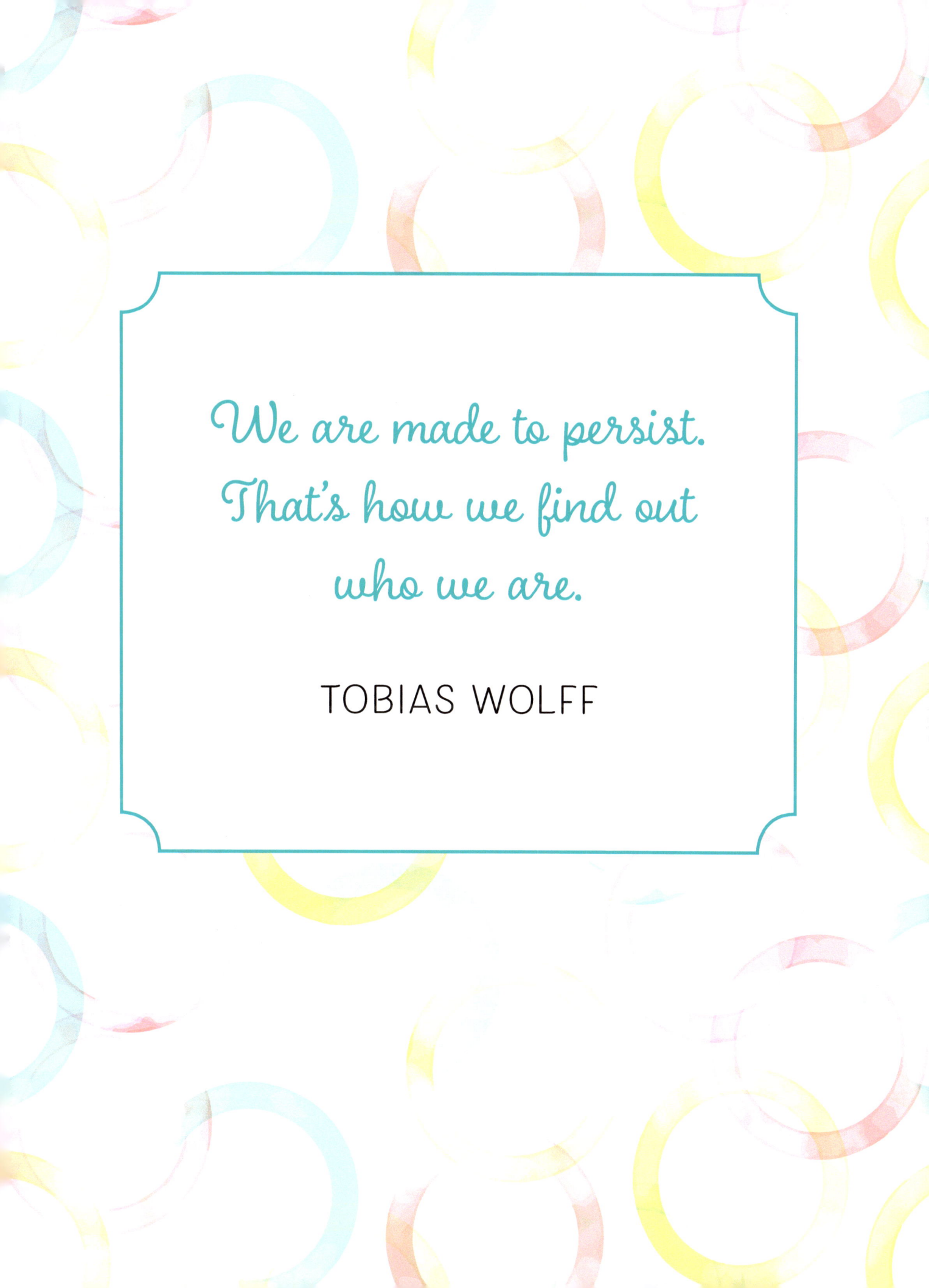

> *We are made to persist. That's how we find out who we are.*
>
> TOBIAS WOLFF

CHAPTER EIGHT
This Too Shall Pass (Part Two)

Thank you, Lord, for another day.

Every once in a while, I wake up on the wrong side of the bed... this was one of those days.

Not only did I not feel well emotionally but physically I felt like a train had run over me. It all started when I awoke and didn't feel up to going to my appointment. I kept dragging myself around my apartment debating whether I was going to cancel or not.

Well, after much fussing and whatnot I decided not to go. Normally I try not to miss appointments if I can help it. For the most part, my health is good so I don't have too many excuses to stay home.

But today... I did. after the physical thing kicked in, the emotional thing kicked in. Bam! I was depressed! ☹

Not to worry, my reader. I pulled out of it, and if you're feeling this way right now as you read this, you can pull out of it too! The first thing I needed to do was change my thought process to one of positivity. I needed self-talk of encouragement to pull myself out of this 'black hole' that I fell into. Ouch!

After two cups of coffee and some self-soothing/self-talk I managed to get up and get dressed. Now, something told me get dressed because 'company was coming.' Sure enough.

Melissa and Kim rang my doorbell. Of course, being in the 'mood' I was in, I was determined not to see anyone today. But lo and behold, Melissa and Kim were just as determined to get in the building to make sure I was 'OK' (it's good to have friends who care and are genuinely concerned about my well-being).

I looked through the peephole and decided to let them in. What a joyful lift for me just having their presence there in my apartment. I no longer felt 'alone' in my worries. I shared with them what was going on and before I knew it, my burden was lifted! The 'boulder' I was carrying around dropped off my shoulders and hit the floor! I was smiling, making eye contact, body language changed, and I felt like a new person.

Thank you, God, for sending Melissa and Kim my way to brighten up my day.

Before I knew it, I was up and out my apartment practically skipping to the library. I had a new 'pep to my step' yes! Everything was going to be 'OK.'

Never leave 'til tomorrow that which you can do today.

BENJAMIN FRANKLIN

CHAPTER NINE
Procrastination

*"Never leave 'til tomorrow
that which you can do today."*
—Benjamin Franklin

I like this quote from Benjamin Franklin. It says it all. Do you tend to procrastinate? Leaving for tomorrow what could be done today? Sad to say, I do... sometimes. I could name a few things that I'm procrastinating on, but I'll do it another time... ☺

Now, let me see, dear reader, if I can add a more 'positive' spin on procrastination, if you will.

There are probably many things that require 'action.' Like today, there are also many things that can't be taken care of 'today' because there is a waiting period or papers need to process. For example, applying to college. You can do the paperwork 'today' but there is a waiting period for acceptance to the college of your choice. There's also waiting for financial aid to come through. This, to me, is not procrastination.

I know from experience. I have done the footwork, now the waiting begins. Maybe the college is procrastinating! ☺

So as far as procrastination... I say: 'do it now'... or... 'just do it.' There are certain things in life that I would like to 'just do or do it now' and get it over with.

For example, paperwork. I take it and do it 'babystep' style. Do a little pile, rest, do some more, have a cup of tea, do some more, rest. You get the general idea.

The thing is to get it done and over with... period.

So next time you want to 'procrastinate'... put it off (pun intended) and just try your best to get started. A little bit at a time... babysteps... yes! Babysteps.

When I stand before
God at the end of my life,
I would hope that I would
not have a single bit of
talent left and could say,
'I used everything
you gave me.'

ERMA BOMBECK

CHAPTER 10
Don't Give Up

Dear special one... I write this to you because I know sometimes you go through a lot and don't know which way to turn, but I say to you... don't give up.

I know there are days when you are filled with anxiety and confusion about what to do, but again, I say to you... don't give up.

I know there are days when you just want to 'isolate' and be by yourself because sometimes, sometimes the pain is just too much to bear, but I say to you... don't give up.

I know there may be days when you want to 'give up' on your life because you feel you can't make it another day... again I say... don't give up.

If you don't give up, you will see the light at the end of the tunnel. Trust me because I, too have felt this way on a day or two, but I have seen the light at the end of the tunnel and it is shining brightly for you and for me.

Go in peace... believe in yourself... know that you can make it in this life. Yes! You can make it!

Your time is limited, so don't waste it living someone else's life.

STEVE JOBS

Acknowledgements

First to my Lord and Savior Jesus Christ for allowing me the privilege of writing this book. I could not have done it without him.

To my publishers, Dawn and Steven Porter of Stillwater River Publications. Many thanks for taking time out of your schedule to meet with me on several occasions to discuss my book. Thank you for your ideas, comments, and support. Dawn and Steven opened Stillwater Books in 2018. They have been publishers since 2012. I also want to thank Dawn for doing the illustrations for my book. Great job! Dawn and Steven's mission statement is to help local authors find an audience for their work.

To Lily 'Ma' Carter. What else can I say but I love you very much. You have been a true friend to me from day one. I am so happy to have you as my 'adopted mom' because you have shown perseverance, love, and patience with me through the years. We have spent countless hours on the phone laughing and, yes, sometimes crying. Your listening skills are phenomenal. Thank you over and over again. May God bless you and your family today and always.

To Tammy Thornber... you are a great friend and have supported me from day one. I look forward to seeing you every day with your smile, and let's not forget the hugs... aww, the hugs. Every time you see me, you would make the time to come and hug me. Thank you for your encouraging words of perseverance to me and your support in writing this book. I am as proud of you as you are of me. May God help and bless you in all your future endeavors.

To Melissa Oliveira, my nurse. I realize you, too, are busy, but took time out to read my manuscript. Thank you. I will never forget our many talks and how well you see that my medical needs are met. We also had many laughs too! Thank you for being there for me when I really needed you. A special 'nurse' you are to me and all people. Keep up the good work! Thanks for being on my team!

To Kimberly Tack, my case manager. I will miss you as you move on to future endeavors. I wish you nothing but the best in all you do in life. Thank you for making sure I get to all my appointments on time with time to spare. We shared many discussions along the way with laughs too! You are a very good case manager and helped me remember things I might have forgotten when I was at my appointments. Come visit us when you have a moment. Thanks for being on my team!

To Gina Diaz, better known as 'Mama D.' Thank you for being you. Your support and words of encouragement mean a lot to me. You work the front desk as a professional at all times. Thank you for the many laughs with personal stories you shared with me. May you forever be blessed, today and always.

To Sandy Oliviera, librarian. Many hours I have spent in the library reading and working on my manuscript. Thank you for always taking time to talk to me on a personal level. Your sense of humor just lifts my spirits. Thank you for getting the books I need and in large print. You are a special person and you socialize with patrons as they come to drop off books or pick up what you have for them. Your smile is contagious. Thank you for all you do at Foxpoint Library for me and others. May God bless you today and always.

To Julie Sabourin, librarian. Thank you too for being there for me with getting the books I need. You have such a quiet spirit about you as you go about your day. We have shared on a personal level about life and I appreciate your listening skills. Your voice is very soothing as you speak softly. You are very friendly with staff and patrons too. Thank you for all you do at Foxpoint Library for me and others. May God bless you today and always.

*Faith tells me that no
matter what lies ahead of me,
God is already there.*

About the Author

Linda is seventh of twelve children. She was raised in New Bedford, Massachusetts, but now lives in Providence, Rhode Island for the last thirty years. She attended the University of Rhode Island with a major in human development and family.

Linda enjoys creative writing and hopes one day to write a children's book. She has written for *Street Sights,* a monthly publication in Providence and the surrounding areas. There is also a write-up about her in the April 2019 issue of *Street Sights.*

Linda also entered a writing contest at Oasis Mental Health Consumer Advocacy in Providence and won first place two years in a row. Also, she entered another writing contest at the University of Rhode Island and won first place.

PHOTO CREDITS

Steve Jobs
Uploaded by segagman on Flickr.com.
https://creativecommons.org/licenses/by/2.0/
Some modifications were made.

Maya Angelou
William J. Clinton Presidential Library.

Tobias Wolff
Uploaded by Tobias_Wolff on Flickr.com.
https://creativecommons.org/licenses/by-sa/2.0/.
Some modifications were made.

Erma Bombeck
Uploaded by Denise Wauters on Flickr.com
https://creativecommons.org/licenses/by/2.0/
Some modifications were made.

Photo of the author by Melissa Oliveira

www.ingramcontent.com/pod-product-compliance
Lightning Source LLC
Chambersburg PA
CBHW060756090426
42736CB00002B/52